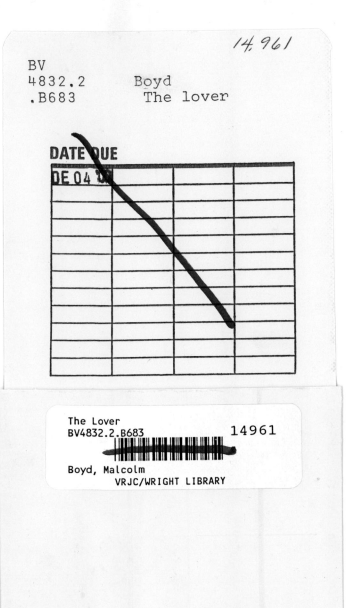

THE LOVER

Other books by Malcolm Boyd:
Crisis in Communication
Christ and Celebrity Gods
Focus
If I Go Down to Hell
The Hunger, The Thirst
Are You Running with Me, Jesus?
Free to Live, Free to Die
Malcolm Boyd's Book of Days
The Fantasy Worlds of Peter Stone and Other Fables
As I Live and Breathe: Stages of an Autobiography
My Fellow Americans
Human Like Me, Jesus

MALCOLM BOYD

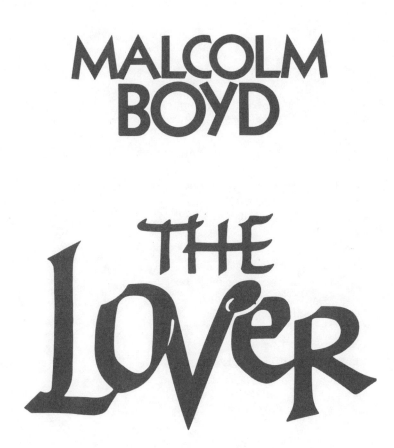

THE LOVER

WORD BOOKS, Publisher
Waco, Texas

THE LOVER

Grateful acknowledgment is extended to the following periodicals in which passages of this book appeared in a different form: *Christianity and Crisis* (November 1, 1971 issue), Copyright © 1971 by Christianity and Crisis, Inc.; *McCall's* magazine (April, 1972 issue); and *The New York Times* (December 12, 1971), © 1971 by The New York Times Company. Reprinted by permission.

First Printing, October, 1972
Second Printing, November, 1972

Printed in the United States of America
Library of Congress catalog card number: 72–84155

TO Dick and Nancy, Bill and Mary, Daniel and Elizabeth, Paul and Jenny, Scott and Muffy, Quinland and Myrtle, John and Patsy, Paul and Kay, Richard and Helen, Big and Peg, Keith and Sheila, Amos and Sally, Mike and Josy, Gordon and Barbara, Ed and Bunchy, Morris and Jean, Arthur and Roberta, Layton and Nan, Bill and Ina, George and Peg, Chet and Mimi, Arthur and Mary Ann, Henri and Gladys, Ted and Bea, John and Esther, Bob and Bobbie, Jeff and Mary, Harold and Betty, Henry and Suzanne, Reginald and Dolores, Roy and Dale, Bill and Vonette, John and Laurie, Jim and Ginger, Ray and Bea, Bonnie and Mike, Dot and Jack, Dick and Helen, Jack and Marion, Bill and Betsy, Hugh and Ruth, and . . .

A<small>N EMERGING AGE RUSHES TO MEET US.</small>

Scientific discoveries, global relationships, technological developments, and new dynamics of the human odyssey move rapidly from the future to the present.

A faith is also emerging. Its vessel is an emerging church whose forms, doctrines, and rituals remain largely unknown.

The emerging faith affirms the power of love and hope. Its deity lives and breathes in the midst of life, and is not an impersonal abstraction, a statue carved out of stone, or a statement of philosophy, yet can be expressed in all of these ways. The emerging faith affirms the existence of mystery and wonder, spiritual and moral meaning within life, and the gospel of love which is the antithesis of any form of terror used against human beings and their environment.

It is tragic and dismaying that in recent history organized religion has heretically participated in the separation of essential meaning from life's realities. *Here,* a dogmatic rule has savaged human sexuality and caused bitter anguish to be suffered by millions of men, women, and children. *There,* the church has openly and disgracefully lived with war, racism, and social ills that irrevocably blighted many more millions of lives.

This heresy practiced by organized religion has cruelly led to the dissociation of God in the minds of many people from human meaning itself. Can the existence of *anything*—regulated work hours, hungry sexuality, election laws, the waging of war, the treatment of minorities, the expansion of trade, the experience of personal loneliness or meaninglessness—be seen as *unrelated* to God? It cannot. Yet the experience of this relationship in people's lives has too often been atomized, largely as a result of the teaching or example set by those who led.

Curiously, they tended either to emphasize academic rationality so that people became ashamed of expressing feeling and repressed it, or else they exercised unrestrained feeling and taught people that intellectual reasoning betrayed a sinful lack of faith. People needed *both* reason and feeling, of course, but many veered off in one extreme direction or the other as a result of their reactions to such teaching, thereby discarding a strongly unified basis for a healthy spiritual life.

So, we have been brought callously and cynically to the point where the coolly unanswered question of our time is: What has anything to do with *anything?* It is a ghastly inscription for a billion tombstones. We have been taught by learned pundits: Leave meaning alone, for it is heady and dangerous stuff. Indeed. It is the stuff of living. The gray absence of meaning underlies present mass ennui and the malaise that rots hope.

A man, a woman, or a child is designed to be a *living* person. Life runs from Sunday morning through Saturday night, falling snow through burning sun, spring leaves through autumn smoke, birth through death, dawn through midnight. *Is* there a faith, or is such talk simply another element in a long list of deceptions? *Is* there a God, or does each one of several ideologically and financially competing "religions" or "churches" have a convenient Rainmaker to perform miracles on call, bury live believers inside a separatist ghetto, and wage a self-righteous war against outside agitation?

I reject both tribal gods and the malaise of human hopelessness. I affirm my belief in The Lover. "If I speak in the tongues of men and of angels, but have not love, I am a noisy gong or a clanging cymbal. And if I have prophetic powers, and understand all mysteries and all knowledge, and if I have all faith, so as to remove mountains, but have not love, I am nothing. If I give away all I have, and if I deliver my body to be

burned, but have not love, I gain nothing. . . .
When I was a child, I spoke like a child, I thought
like a child, I reasoned like a child; when I became a man, I gave up childish ways. For now we
see in a mirror dimly, but then face to face. Now
I know in part; then I shall understand fully,
even as I have been fully understood. So faith,
hope, love abide, these three; but the greatest of
these is love."

I speak subjectively and objectively, pro-
phetically and mystically, evangelistically and
secularly, about The Lover. The Lover is holier
than human, and boundlessly free as compared
with our chains and limitations. The Lover is
capable of actions of great power, although these
are never grossly magical but clearly visible to
eyes of faith. The Lover understands intimately
the longings and workings of the human body-
mind-soul. The Lover offers a gospel unifying
justice, judgment, faith, and hope. The Lover is
eternal in the sense of transforming the present
into deeper, transcendent, and lasting reality.

I participate in creating, shaping, and supporting the emerging church. It is more than
a bureaucracy of grinding machinery, traditions
that have become idols, or rules that take pre-
cedence over human lives. Its gospel is neither

fundamentalist nor social, but the gospel of love.

I affirm The Lover's name, celebrate The Lover's presence, share with other people The Lover's gospel, and seek in communion with The Lover to become a lover.

I

I MAY BE HAPPY OR SAD, FILLED WITH ENTHUSIASM OR UTTERLY WITHOUT HOPE.

I MAY LOVE OR HATE. I MAY SEEK ANSWERS OR REJECT HELP. I MAY RESPOND TO THE LOVER'S PRESENCE OR REMAIN INDIFFERENT. YET THE LOVER REMAINS CONSTANT AND IS ALWAYS WITH ME. I KNOW THAT I AM LOVED.

SMOKE WAS RISING IN THE AIR FROM BURNING LEAVES.

It seemed as if my old life had been placed on top of the leaves. Would it burn furiously until it had become a simple and pure spirit of smoke?

Although sunlight penetrated the atmosphere of that chilled autumn morning, it brought no warmth to the trees, to fallen leaves, or to me.

In a few hours, I would go away, never to return unless I wished to revisit buildings and memories. But now, in this instant, I was still present in the place. It had not just yet been reduced to a memory. The reality was immediate, pressing with iron persistence against consciousness. I felt drained of emotion, yet intense feeling permeated every pore and muscle of my flesh.

I smelled the smoke. My meditation was, in effect, the confrontation of an immediate reality —The Lover.

M<small>Y FACE FELT FROZEN IN THE ICY WIND.</small>

Must I wear this mask forever?

I was a young student, walking along the wintry streets of the city, twenty blocks, two hundred blocks, the pattern of falling snow hypnotically softening my vision. I felt no immediate connection with anyone or anything. The vast stone canyons were characterless. A light shining in a distant window mocked me.

A machine filled with people surged up the street, then abruptly turned the corner. A body approached mine and, treading on ice, walked through a doorway. I had no route or destination, yet hurried. The city closed in upon me, its long street strangling me with the tenacity of a soiled scarf. I ran harder and harder to escape. My search deepened. I asked myself: If I found home, could I recognize it? Amid this anxiety and desperation I recognized The Lover.

I DROVE THE CAR FASTER.

My foot pushed the accelerator to the floor. I would obliterate an hour of the granite rock of time.

In the distance I could see a truck coming closer in the opposite lane. It was big and moving fast. Just then I got hemmed in by a slow sedan that had turned onto the highway directly in front of me from a dirt road.

My time was being hacked away. That time, holy and untouchable, was all I seemed to have in the world at that precise moment.

I gunned the motor, swerving my car out into the opposite lane. The big truck was just ahead and racing head-on toward me. The sedan seemed to gain speed. I gambled on a few inches of distance and blew it all. The car wheel held in my hand was shaking.

When I passed the sedan and turned back into the right lane ahead of it, I felt my car almost brush the steel hulk of the leviathan truck.

Suddenly I was scared. Death had come close. It terrified me that I was running so fast. I asked The Lover: What was I running away from in terror and speed?

WHITE SHEETS WERE CRUMPLED ON THE HEAVY MAHOG-
ANY BED.

My grandfather who lay on it was dying. A tall and commanding man, he had been suffering from cancer for a long while, so his death was expected.

His family stood around the room watching him die. My grandmother held one of his hands. The doctor stood by him on the other side of the bed.

I was far, far back in the room, barely inside the door—was I supposed to be there at all?— standing on my toes trying to see my grandfather over an obtrusive adult shoulder. I was a young boy who had not yet seen anyone die.

I thought that grandpa looked very pale as he lay still on the bed. I wanted to run across the room and ask him to get up, hold me on his lap, and tell me a story. We were pals, grandpa and I, and I loved going places with him. He always introduced me to people, and I was proud.

Suddenly, I heard an awful sound like a rattle. My grandfather seemed to be having trouble with his breathing. Soon I saw the doctor reach over and pull down his eyelids. My grandmother put her head down on the bed, and her body shook when she cried.

I ducked outside the door and ran as fast as I could down the stairs. Opening the front door of the house, I walked swiftly up the street. I knew that grandpa was dead and I would not be able to see him again, but it was very difficult to sort this out in my mind.

MY SOUL IS REFRESHED.

I am grateful, for my life had become absurdly flat and dimensionless. It lacked humor and grace. My feelings had dried out.

This coming of spring has brought memories flooding in. I am surprised and delighted that in this moment I feel no regret. Yes, I am grateful for everything that has happened to me, everybody whom I have known, all that I have done. These are my life.

The future greets me in swiftly passing moments, including this one. I am curious. Oh, may the power of love fill me with the sweet anguish of caring deeply about life.

I LOOKED DOWN AT A HANDFUL OF LIGHTS IN THE DARK-
NESS.

I was flying on a plane. Once again, I was
being uprooted, torn mercilessly from any security
and moorings that I knew.

The plane had been in the air for fifteen
minutes. The seat belt sign had gone off. The long
flight was at last under way. Holding my face
against the cold glass of the window, I looked
down at a small town momentarily visible in the
night darkness.

I wondered how much change and hurt the
human mechanism can bear. I told myself that
my heart was not on this plane. Could life be
simply a macabre drama in which one had no
choice but to play bravely the part he was as-
signed? Soon I fell asleep.

When I awakened, the plane was landing. I
had reached my destination. Soon I made new
friends in a new place and learned to do a new
kind of work. Then I realized that my heart had
indeed been on the plane. I was still carrying it
about inside me. I had successfully transported
myself, heart and all, from one place in the world
to another.

I SENSE A NEW BEGINNING.

Weariness and languor of spirit had replaced my enthusiasm. I hated to feel hopeless, yet I sometimes felt that way.

But now there is a stirring of hope inside my life again. I am able to look away simply from spiritual stagnation and a lack of vigor within my soul. The Lover beckons to me and I am grateful.

Unrelieved gray is slowly changing into the refreshing ambience of greens, reds, and yellows. A sense of anticipation has overcome my listlessness and depression. I behold inner beauty where I saw only ugliness. Happiness catches me unprepared, and I can laugh out loud. The Lover tugs at my soul.

Wʜᴏ ɪs ᴍʏ ɴᴇɪɢʜʙᴏʀ?

I was taught as a child that it is the person who lives next door. But then I had to ask, did that person cease to be my neighbor by the simple act of moving away? I began wondering if someone living as far away as the next block could be my neighbor. Could someone in the next town, or a city five thousand or even fifty thousand miles away, be my neighbor?

Growing up, I learned that my neighbor is both highly specific and legion. He lives next door or halfway around the world. He shares my values or utterly opposes them. He resembles me or looks completely different.

But if my neighbor, whoever or wherever he may be, is persecuted for his beliefs, am I not persecuted, too? If my neighbor's humanity is called into question, is not my humanity called into question, too? The Lover dwells in my neighbor as he dwells in me.

II

O<small>N MY TRAVELS I HAVE DISCOVERED THAT I AM USUALLY MAKING TWO SIMULTANEOUS JOURNEYS.</small>

> ONE IS OUTSIDE MYSELF, AS MY EYES SEARCH LAND-SCAPES THROUGH TRAIN, PLANE, OR CAR WINDOWS, AND I PERHAPS CHAT WITH OTHER PASSENGERS. THE OTHER IS INSIDE MYSELF, WHERE DREAMS COLLIDE WITH FACTS, LONELINESS GRAPPLES WITH AN URGE TO SEEK RELATIONSHIPS, AND THE QUES-TION OF MY REAL IDENTITY OVERPOWERINGLY AS-SERTS ITSELF. THE LOVER IS A FELLOW VOYAGER ON THE JOURNEYS INSIDE MYSELF.

I STOOD FOR A TIME BY AN OCEAN.

Fog hung loosely over the beach. Near the shore the sea was veined marble. Farther out, it turned dull green and finally gray. Seven sea gulls flew closely over the surface while a single bird casually rode the waves. Foam made a pattern on the water that resembled Spanish lace.

A cliff guarding the shore had a jagged gash in it. The sea battered the cliff, attacking with fury. The sound of the sea was a constant roar that built to a crescendo when it struck big rocks below the cliff. But the rocks remained secure despite the ocean's relentless onslaught. One rock was washed by water five times each minute. Would this go on forever? Indeed, could this be a picture of hell—or heaven?

Buchenwald. Auschwitz. Dachau. Bergen-Belsen. Lwow-Janowska.

The names of the death camps where six million Jews perished in the Nazi holocaust are written inside Yad Vashem in Jerusalem. Ashes of victims' bodies were brought here from the camps. A flame burns by the grave.

It is quiet inside Yad Vashem this morning except for some children's voices that can be heard from the outside and the sound of footsteps on the stone ramp by the grave.

I cannot grasp the monstrous thing that is memorialized here, yet I must try.

Outside, near the symbol of a concentration camp smokestack, I read these words, "Now and forever in memory of those who rebelled in the camps and ghettos, fought in the woods, in the underground, and with the Allied Forces, who braved their way to Eretz Israel and those who died sanctifying the name of God."

Laughing Jewish children run past me on this sunny day in Israel. After the crucifixion of the holocaust, they are the new life that has sprung into being.

PICASSO'S "PROFILE" CAST IN CONCRETE STANDS EXPOSED TO THE WIND, SUN, AND RAIN IN THE OUTDOOR GARDEN OF THE ISRAEL MUSEUM IN JERUSALEM.

I walk around the "Profile." Now I stand looking up through a gaping hole in it toward the sun which is occasionally hidden beneath a dark cloud before it shines again. When I bring my eyes closer to the earth, I see three other works of art nearby. To my right is the figure of Prometheus. Straight ahead is what appears to be a bizarre instrument of tension or war. To my left is a metal screen.

The wind blows hard. Trees dance. A woman moves in the distance. The skeletons of new apartment buildings take up space in the sky. When I look straight up to the top of Picasso's work that stands against the driving clouds in the Jerusalem sky, it seems to be falling down, and so do I.

I am human and a part of stone, air, and space. My soul expands. Picasso's concrete "Profile" appears to have a firmer grip on space than I do. Will its body outlive mine? But I know that my soul is the stronger.

It IS MIDNIGHT IN JERUSALEM.

At the Western (Wailing) Wall, bright lights illumine its ancient stones. Pigeons nest in some of the cracks that appear in the façade. Notes that people have written, many of them prayers to God, are lodged in holes in the rocks.

A lone figure dressed in black sits before the wall. He chants, reading aloud in Hebrew from a prayer book. His voice rises and falls in a rhythmic pattern.

The wall is naked. The Temple that once stood inside the wall has long been destroyed. It seems to me that the pock-marked stones of the Wailing Wall witness to the eternal temple that dwells in human hearts.

For some city folk a sunrise is not available except as a thin line between encroaching buildings.

Once I visited friends who lived on the desert in Arizona. I decided that I would get up at 5 A.M. to watch the sun rise. The next morning, as I walked across the desert, my footsteps seemed to be the only ones on earth. I approached a gulch, climbing down a hill past cactus plants and immense rocks. A bird laughed mockingly in the distance, while close by another chirped incessantly. I reached out to touch a worn, gnarled, and intricately twisted plant that seemed made of driftwood. Nearby stood a saguaro which had already witnessed 60,000 sunrises.

Light from the invisible sun illumined scattered clouds in the sky, transforming them from pearl to silver. A grotesque rock, shaped like a stolid Goya figure obsessed by fury or zeal, leaned toward the sun as its rim came close to the horizon.

Suddenly the sun burst forth. It was blinding. All I could discern was an immeasurable, hot, and dazzling source of energy. Meditating in the quiet of the early morning, I stood near a green lace-patterned plant. It was consumed when caught by the fire of the rising sun, seeming itself to be a blinding source of energy.

I was both humbled and affirmed, for I belonged there (in my transitory human state) as well as the saguaro or the lace-patterned plant.

A TIDAL WAVE OF LIGHTS CONFRONTED ME.

Driving my car at night onto a crowded Los Angeles freeway, I jumped in between a speeding sports car and a giant truck. The roaring flood of sound and glow consumed me.

To my left a hillside community, reflected by lights in a thousand homes, appeared and quickly vanished. To my right a university campus came into view and almost immediately evaporated into the night air. Behind tall trees I glimpsed an empty lighted street that resembled an unused motion picture backlot late at night.

Now I sped ahead encased between solid, fast moving lines of color and steel in a middle lane. Each car around me was like a distant planet in its remoteness, brilliance, and impersonality. Whether I caught a fleeting glimpse of a human being inside a car or at one of a montage of curtained apartment house windows overlooking the freeway, there was an absence of flesh and spirit relationship. People seemed to withdraw furtively into their own tiny bit of space, as if they were burrowing ever deeper into nonexistent soil for protection from each other. One was as unnoticed, forgotten, and anonymous on this freeway as a person standing naked at an open window in a huge building complex.

Locked into this purely functional existence, my mind wandered, then drifted away. Boredom became a numbing experience. I engineered my speeding vehicle over the cement floor of an encroaching wasteland.

In MADRID, ON A RAINY MORNING, I SAW DEATH (MY OWN) IN MY MIND'S EYE.

I was not afraid of it; I was not being morbid; I simply looked at it. The hiss of car tires running over the wet pavement outside came through the open window of my room. Sharp horns tooted shrilly in the distance, yet seemed close. The steady muted whirr of motors slowly penetrated my consciousness.

I climbed out of bed to look through the window at people outside. They were scurrying along the drenched streets, their black umbrellas bent by the wind. The smell of the fresh rain now filled my room. My mind seemed to be drenched. Didn't I see myself out there on the street, running forever in the midst of a crowd of people?

I wondered for a moment if the present had become eternity.

During a visit to Venice I was awakened by sounds on the canal.

Jumping out of bed, I looked through the window of my room. Barges filled with men and merchandise were moving along the water. Waves washed the stone steps of an old palace.

I wondered: Is Venice simply a stage setting? In my imagination, I could see lights sending reflections of colors across the canal on a night four hundred years ago. A gondola was carrying home a Doge's emissary from a state meeting, but, alas, a frightful scene was about to be enacted. The barge was waylaid by sturdy men in masks who had slipped through the night fog in other gondolas. The emissary was murdered with sharp knives stolen from Constantinople.

Now, under the bright morning sun, I could see the colors of a palace emerge from the old stone: rose, pink, and faded orange. Looking for human faces in the canal barges, I was suddenly (in meditation) confronted by an array of Byzantine masks.

Who can speak of permanence? Who can dogmatically define security? Are we not all like the Venetians, sinking slowly beneath gentle yet relentless waves? Death is a reality in each of our lives.

FLORENCE HAD NOT FULLY AWAKENED.

I walked along the Arno River where a few men and boys, standing on the shore or seated in stationary rowboats, were already fishing. One man's dog slept peacefully alongside his master. A man came running along the river, which reflected his figure but blurred it with ripples.

I walked toward the cathedral. Inside its uncluttered space, I experienced a sense of delight. I could breathe and think and feel as if I were not bound by the limitations of walls and a roof. The cathedral seemed less a divine arsenal than a peaceful garden, a symbol of man's reverence for life.

In CZECHOSLOVAKIA I FELT AN EXUBERANT SENSE OF AN-
TICIPATION.

I could see it in the way people walked on the
street. Although there was repression and danger,
smiles were stronger than worn anxious creases
in people's faces.

Flowers were for sale at street corners. The
sun ricocheted off stone walls and iron window
bars. A spirit called to a reborn spirit within
people to awaken, laugh, think, create, and make
changes in life.

Soon afterwards I felt sad, betrayed, and lost.
Then I came to realize that The Lover's spirit
was not dead. It was only hiding, working myste-
riously in secret places of men's souls and hopes.

Trees and I converse.

On a hilltop near Yale University in Connecticut three favorite trees of mine stand close together. The first is immense, and parts of its wooden roots thrust above the ground seem to be made of steel. Two baleful but secretly loving eyes peer at one from a sturdy trunk. In winter our conversations have taken place in snowdrifts. In summer I must walk beneath thick clusters of its leaves, deep green shapes that turn to copper when illumined by strong sunlight, in order to sit by a friend.

The second tree is not so grand, indeed, it is quite plain. I believe that it is probably the average tree. It is neatly proportioned, it has been reproduced in a thousand drawings; one is greeted always by graceful familiarity and pleasant charm that knows neither moods nor temperament.

Utterly different is the third tree which is a bewitching prima donna. Her shape, when bereft of lavish foliage amid winter ice, retains its poised lines—a bare hint of ancient aristocratic madness and absolute beauty. Its summer leaves present a vision of costumed glory, and one pays homage.

These three friends never betray my trust, engage in idle gossip about me, or cause me pain. They are older than I am and will doubtless outlive me. I respect their wisdom; they forgive my youth.

I CANNOT ALWAYS MEDITATE PROFOUNDLY.

I must confess that I often fail to take giant strides forward upon my existential journey at precisely those moments when I had planned to do so. I recall a recent visit to a charming house in a romantic forest in a distant land. It was the dead of night when I awakened, moved about the house, and sought to commune with the expanse of nature surrounding me.

I could hear the victory salvo of a thousand crickets that had just seized the castle. The only light I could perceive was cast by a sliver of a new moon. A dog slept unperturbed as if he were a porcelain doorstop that breathed. It was a seductive moment to putter about in my mind and soul. Resolutely, I set myself to philosophizing about important matters of life and death.

But then my humanity overtook me. Yawning and blinking wearily, I fell off to sleep. The journeys inside myself had stopped for the night.

III

THE LOVER HAS CRIED WITH ME, LAUGHED WITH ME; AC-
CEPTED ME, CHANGED ME; FORGIVEN ME, ASKED
ME TO FORGIVE OTHERS.

GRAY LOCKERS LINED THE LONG CORRIDORS.

I saw them on that first day when I started attending high school. They made the old building, with its loud ringing bells and intricate set of rules, seem even more a prison than it was.

In that vast new world of the high school I knew only one human being—a boy who had been a close friend of mine one year earlier in another city. He had written me that he would enroll today in this same school.

I searched for John everywhere but could only find an army of impersonal and unknown faces. Suddenly I saw John's familiar face. I shouted a greeting and ran toward him through a crowd of students. It seemed odd that he did not turn his head to indicate that he had heard my voice.

Then I placed my hand upon his shoulder. John looked at me for a moment with what seemed to be cold hate. Abruptly he turned away and walked ahead. I followed. I asked him what was the matter. I said that I could not understand his action. He kept on walking, leaving me behind.

After my initial experience of searing hurt, I quickly rationalized his rejection in the interest of my own self-esteem. Soon I partially came to understand the incident, in at least a surface sense, as meaning that it was I who had somehow rejected John. Yet this feeling did not really penetrate deeply. My hurt remained. We never spoke to each other again. I did not continue to think about it at any conscious level.

But what had prompted John's action? I wondered if his family had some unknown religious or cultural prejudice toward me and whether his mother or father forbade our friendship. Or had I perhaps deeply hurt John in a youthful way that I did not understand?

This was my first hard lesson in the mysteries of friendship.

I WANT TO SHIFT THE PIECES OF MY LIFE.

Some of them are holding me down so that I cannot move. Others are hurting me. I feel that I am stifled and cannot easily get my breath. I am sad, making everybody near me miserable or confused.

I keep trying to move these giant weights in my life. Suddenly I realize that my life has become cumbersome and crowded, as if it were a room filled with too many heavy pieces of immovable furniture.

I want to see open hope in the place of endless clutter that obscures my vision and regain perspective so that I can balance the awareness of tragedy with joyful discovery. I am tired unto death of my cynicism, bitterness, and feeling that life is not going anywhere except in circles that are predictable and inhuman.

I want to laugh out loud, look at a streaked white cloud in the sky that resembles a falling angel, behold wonder in the morning, shake with love, and feel consumed by joy. Can the stuck pieces within my life break loose?

I want to turn around.

W<small>E WERE IN SEARCH OF A GHOST.</small>

It was a moonlit Halloween night. We drove to the outskirts of the town to visit the haunted house of Count Arhyaz. No one knew if Count Arhyaz had ever actually existed, but according to local folklore his house turned into a ghost-packed castle at night. He was supposed to haunt the place.

My three friends and I—all of us were students in the same high school—walked around the stone wall surrounding the old house. Did a single light flicker in an upstairs window? The night was deathly quiet.

Shortly past midnight, we hoisted our bodies over the ivy covered wall into a weed-filled remnant of a garden. The gaunt branches of a tree, heavy with dead leaves, reached ominously toward us. I bumped into a stone bird bath. The air was frigid, and our bodies grew cold as we ran from bush to bush, tree to tree, drawing closer to the house.

A local legend told about a gigantic hound dog that ran wild in the garden at night. The maddened mastiff was supposed to tear to pieces anyone who entered the grounds. Did we hear the baying of the great dog under the half-moon?

Now we stood in the frozen air outside the back door of Count Arhyaz's castle. A twig cracked underfoot. Afterwards all of us vividly remembered Count Arhyaz's face, bloodless and whiter than snow. Didn't he stretch out his hand and start walking toward us? I would swear for years to come that he resembled Frankenstein.

Propelling our bodies in manic high energy across dead leaves, we cried and shouted in desperate fear. Then we thrust ourselves over the wall, ran to our car which had taken on the appearance of a hearse in the moonlight, and drove furiously away.

Over cups of hot chocolate at a diner in the town, we did not talk to each other, but sat in a booth shivering from the cold and memories. Ghosts rattled around beneath our consciousness, refusing to come out and talk in the spacious and warm room where the electric lights blazed.

IT HAPPENED WITHOUT ANY WARNING.

Yesterday I was supremely happy. I seemed to be on a roller coaster, taking all highs. I was animated, enthused, hopeful, creative, and open to the world.

Today that mood is only a distant and complex memory. I do not have the energy or spirit to make the slightest mental or physical exertion. Depression is upon me like a thick cloud. I neither hope nor care about anything.

No one else knows the gargantuan load that is upon me. If I take the slightest step or accomplish an absurdly small task, the effort taxes my whole being.

THE TRAIN WHISTLE BLEW.

I could feel its reverberations inside the old station and inside my flesh and bones. It seemed that I was being called to judgment.

The moment was a terrifying and hopeful one at the same time. I was going away to school. My trunk and two suitcases were already on the train. In a moment, after I had said good-by once again, I would join them.

But what awaited me out there in the vast world? I did not know. Surely there would be new people, new situations, a new environment, new problems, and new definitions. I would grow up.

Now departure and judgment were biting at my heels, as I climbed the blackened steps of the already moving train. How little I knew of life that lay ahead. Why can't anyone ever tell anybody?

IT IS AN UNQUIET DAY IN MY MIND.

Blowing winds obliterate all other sounds. Warm air beneath a hot sun makes my thoughts sweat. My consciousness is ringed by thick foliage hiding angry birds and hungry animals.

What can I do? There is no peace here. Memories do battle with hopes. Fears leap out without warning from behind painful hurts.

I do not like this war inside me.

I WAS A RAMBUNCTIOUS HIGH-SCHOOL STUDENT VISITING CHICAGO WITH A BUDDY DURING SUMMER VACATION.

On our second night, after eating an eight course Italian dinner, we wandered around the Loop. A bright neon sign outside a theater announced an M.G.M. movie about Stanley and Livingstone in the African jungle. We decided to see it.

We settled ourselves contentedly in the theater balcony. However, I had apparently eaten one or two rich dinner courses too many and soon became aware that I was going to be sick. Yet I delayed my departure, for I was enjoying the movie and did not want to miss any of it.

When Spencer Tracy said, "Dr. Livingstone, I presume," I knew that I must go. I turned to Gene, my buddy, in order to excuse myself. He was wearing a brand new brown gabardine suit. Too late, I realized that the sickness was upon me.

Trying to spare Gene, I turned my head away. The people seated in the row directly ahead leaped to their feet, struggling to escape. Cries and the sound of rushing feet drowned out Stanley and Livingstone. People seated on the main floor of the theater looked apprehensively in the direction of the uproar taking place in the balcony.

Nausea overcame me again. This served to increase the fury of people seeking vainly to escape from me. Finally, Gene and I made our leprous way past sullen, uniformed ushers toward the theater lobby with its crystal chandeliers and red carpet. Awaiting us was a procession of defeat past the brilliantly lit box office.

I braced my shoulders for an embarrassing confrontation with the pretty, smiling cashier who sat inside the box office. Several hundred people stood in line before it. As Gene and I engineered our exit, nausea swept over me for the final time that night. I violated the mosaic floor of the movie holy of holies. Consternation broke its bonds.

Gene and I fled up the crowded street of the Loop with the alacrity of pickpockets, the zeal of converts.

THE COLORS WERE DAZZLING.

They were in jewels, and I was in a room filled with them. Some of the people wearing them were famous. The party was elegant.

However, a spiritual emptiness inside that room was a hungry, screaming animal. Men and women struggled painfully to be comfortable within the hard confines of an unyielding pattern that had been meticulously choreographed.

People seemed to limit their own humanness at every turn. No new face could easily break into that tight circle of people who were energetically boring each other to death.

Money spoke loudly. Fame spoke deafeningly. The yearning for human meaning whispered softly but could scarcely be asserted over the din.

I T WAS A SUNLESS, CHILLY MORNING AT THE SUMMER RESORT.

Where there had been an habitual golden aura, now a sullen indefinable grayness filled spaces. The water looked simply cold. Flowers lacked a focus for the direction of their looking. People slept late.

Everything was on edge, out of sorts, and clearly wrong. Security collapsed when habit did. People wondered what they could believe in when the sun did not shine, as it was supposed to do.

When the sun came out at noon, all anxiety was instantly forgotten. The warmth of the sun dissipated every kind of chill. But I wondered how real is casual faith.

I KEEP HEARING OF OTHER PEOPLE'S DEATHS.

"His brother died."

"Did you know Denise? She died in New York."

"Bruce was killed in the war."

"Of course, you heard that Ann died in Europe."

I know the day must come when it is my death that is announced. It seems strange that I will not be able to talk about it, for I have never liked to be left out.

There must be good ways to prepare for one's death, yet I seem always to be busy doing other things. There are other people taking up my time and energy with their ideas, personalities, and problems. At just the moment when I might be able to sit down alone and soberly ponder decisions to be made concerning my death, I find that I am too tired to think about it.

Right now I need to think about this day, someone whom I love, and a task that lies ahead.

IV

THE LOVER HAS MOVED THROUGH THE WALLS OF MANY PEOPLE'S LIVES WITH ME.

SOME OF THESE MEN AND WOMEN ARE CONFRONTED BY ANXIETY, PAIN, AND AT TIMES A SENSE OF HOPELESSNESS. THE LOVER TEACHES ME: ALL OF THESE PEOPLE ARE LOVED AS I AM.

IRENE GOT OUT OF BED ONLY A HALF HOUR AGO.

Last night, she sat up until 2 A.M. watching an old movie on TV. Then she listened for a while to a radio show for night people.

Now she's had her first two cups of coffee and is out in the yard in front of her house, methodically sweeping the stone walk. She is wearing a print housecoat and flat, soiled white shoes.

In a little while Irene will look at a daytime show that she never misses on TV. During the remainder of the day she will switch channels for her favorite shows. The only time she will go out is for a visit to John's Market where she needs to buy corn flakes, ground round, and frozen peas.

Irene never goes outside the house after dark. She's afraid because she lives alone and has heard that crime is rapidly moving to the suburb from the inner city. She smokes two packs of cigarettes a day although she's tried to stop and is down a pack from last year. On Sundays she sees her son and his wife when they come over for a visit.

She has swept the walk all the way to the sidewalk.

DON'T SAY LOVE," PHILIP SAID.

He is seated inside the student union of the commuter college that he attends.

Philip is upper-middle-class, white, unsure of a life's work that would interest him, and has two appointments each week with a psychiatrist who also treats both his father and mother.

"What is important is when you feel close to someone," he said. "This can be just one time or for a long time. If it's for a long time, you should live together. I see no point in marriage unless you feel insecure and in need of that social sanction for your relationship. The toughest question really is how to handle your body. Not your mind or soul. What to do with your meat. Love has no meaning for me. I don't know what it is."

Will Philip come to know that he is loved, and that The Lover is actively engaged in all of his life?

THE BOY IS GOING INTO A TRIPLE-FEATURE MOVIE.

He is ten years old. All that he seems to own in the world is the admission to the Rivoli Theater. He can sit inside the dark make-believe emptiness for hours and see John Wayne, Jane Fonda, Mia Farrow, and Dustin Hoffman. Or would he rather sleep?

His parents have been fighting again and now his dad has angrily left their slum apartment. His mom is drunk, and his grandmother gave him money to get out of everybody's way for the rest of the day.

His eyes look very old.

H<small>E'S WALKING HIS DOG TO THE PARK.</small>

Fifteen years ago, when he retired, he had a heart condition and a very bad drinking problem. Now he's in better health and on the wagon.

He and his small black dog come slowly toward the park entrance. The park is a green oasis off this boulevard of steel buildings. He's wearing a plaid shirt and a gray cap.

Inside the park an elderly woman sits on a bench reading a paperback novel. In the distance a young man wearing a sweatshirt and pants runs around a track.

The man walking his dog looks forward to this outing in the park. He lives with his son and daughter-in-law. His wife died nine years ago and he can't manage alone.

The rage and longing of his drinking days seem to be part of someone else's life. There was something eating at the center of his existence. He couldn't do anything about it but give it food and drink. It went away one day, vanishing like smoke after a fire.

He is laughing. Does he notice The Lover?

THE CHURCH FUND RAISING DRIVE IS IN FULL SWING.

A hard working businessman with good connections accepted the chairmanship. A rich and socially important woman was asked to serve as his assistant.

The new church shouldn't cost a penny over $300,000, everybody was told. The copper roof, of course, must be an expensive one. Yet church leaders believed that the time had come for them to expand within this community, extending both visibility and influence. Surely the social and cultural prestige of a striking new building would be felt immediately, attracting new people to join the congregation.

However, there is a difficult problem to be confronted. The present minister does not fit into the church's plans. His wife is seen as plain, even dowdy in appearance, and something of a distinct social embarrassment. The minister himself is criticized for being out of fashion and, yes, one hears from critics that he is overly pious for a sophisticated community like this one. Nobody questions his sincerity but people whisper that his sermons are too long, he simply doesn't attract the right people, and he seems irritatingly intense concerning social issues that nobody wants to hear about.

The fund raising drive will conclude two weeks from next Saturday night with a mammoth dinner party at the country club. Nobody has asked The Lover.

ELLEN LIKES TO SAY THAT SHE IS YOUNG, GIFTED, AND BLACK.

She graduated last June from an important university where she received her master's degree. She is working now in a well paid and personally rewarding job for a social agency.

Life excites her. It seems all ahead of her, unlimited in scope and intensity. She has taken a small apartment by herself and has begun to furnish it. Men naturally like her. She has a dozen different alternatives for what to do with her life.

She is walking toward me on the street. Her suit is very smart. She wears a leather purse over her shoulder.

Ellen is already middle-class, although her parents and two brothers are not. Ellen's world is split down the middle.

On one side are her parents in their inner-city home, her brothers' jive talk and futile attempts to make a success, her understanding of the meaning of black human experience, and a dim awareness that she might sometime have to make a decision between black and white life styles.

On the other side of her world are white friendships and connections, book clubs, suburban homes, new cars, and a sense of goals dependent only upon the amount of personal effort that is expended.

Ellen in her split world is passing me on the street.

Jon is reading a book in his dormitory room.

He feels as if there were at least six generations between him and students in the high school which he attended before entering this college.

Jon sees a complex of problems awaiting him. Speaking very seriously, he expresses the basic dilemma in this way, "How can you make paths in space? You see, you can't fill it. I used to think life was neatly patterned. It isn't. It is organic. It smells."

What worries Jon the most about the future? "What is most horrifying is when there seem to be no options at all. You have absolutely no choice as to what is going to happen to you."

I wondered: Will Jon come to share The Lover's vision of life, with its open choices and unexpected alternatives?

Louise has a moneyed look.

Louise also has money. She's on most of the art museum, symphony, and hospital boards in the city but seldom goes to their meetings. She just writes checks.

She's here in the shopping center because she wants to make some purchases at the bookstore when it opens. A fountain plays in the mall. On both sides of it she can see the procession of fancy shops that sell clothes, fine silver, glassware, books, gourmet foods, television sets, imported wines, and pet supplies. The men she sees here either work in stores or seem, from her viewpoint, to resemble overcooked vegetables. She watches stout women crowding into the candy store with its rows of dark and cream chocolates and a counter where they can buy extra thick milkshakes topped with whipped cream and a candied cherry.

Louise wishes that she were not so bored. The worst moment in her day seems to be the first one in the morning when she is confronted harshly by the fact that she has simply not got anything to do that she cares about strongly. She has discussed this with physicians and therapists. They gave her pills and advice but nothing changed the situation.

She must buy a new suit for a trip she and Alex will take to Jamaica. Her prayer cell meets this afternoon. She and Alex are going to have dinner tonight at the club with the Dooleys. Louise pops a tranquilizer.

THE SANITATION TRUCK IS SLOWLY MOVING UP THE STREET. Everybody has placed filled garbage cans and bags of trash neatly in front of all the houses on the block. It is Thursday morning when the sanitation department men come on schedule to collect the trash.

The truck is now in front of the Abbots' house. Inside, Ruth Abbot is watching her favorite morning television show get ready to sign off for another day. She must change the beds, make a trip to the laundromat, stop at the post office to mail a package, and hurry to meet Connie Aristedes for lunch at one o'clock.

The sanitation truck was at first just a familiar hum in the distance as it started up the street toward Ruth Abbot's house. Now its whirr is drowning out her favorite TV host.

The four sanitation men outside have glanced in passing at her well-kept lawn, emptied the garbage with a clatter of tin cans, and moved on to the redwood house next door. They move quickly and efficiently.

These four men are the only black people in the neighborhood.

Daphne is at her hairdresser's.

This morning when she got up all the pain of Jack's death suddenly poured in upon her, and she felt that she couldn't stand it. He died seven months ago. She says that she is a mature adult who should have long ago been able to adjust.

But that illusion got knocked in the head along with so many others. She and Jack were a happily married couple. Daphne had often thought she should pinch herself to see if such a thing were really true and happening to her. It was. The same thing had to be said afterwards of Jack's dying.

Anyway this morning she decided after two cups of unsatisfying instant coffee—why bother to make it right just for herself?—that she'd had it. What to do? But her hairdresser's appointment was on the agenda. She would try to think after that.

Getting here, the mood of the place lifted her right away. It was all up—the humor, the lift in her appearance, the chance to talk and be understood.

It's a new experience not having the man she wants in her life. She knows this experience won't go away. But she has decided that she must try to keep busier and work harder than she has done before.

She wonders: Will she learn to accept realities with both patience and determination to change what she can? And can she hasten toward real goals instead of simply trying to lose herself in activity?

PAUL WORKS IN A HAMBURGER JOINT.

The place is open twenty-four hours each day. Paul goes to work at nine o'clock in the morning. He is waiting on a customer now. He also grills burgers, fries eggs, and pours a lot of coffee.

He doesn't make any connections here, but waits to visit a gay bar in the afternoons.

Paul isn't handsome, but he is lean and wiry. His smile is warm. He lives a few blocks away in a dilapidated hotel room that looks out upon an alley.

Sometimes he makes love with an intern from the hospital who stops by the bar late in the evening. They go either to the intern's place or his. Paul met an insurance executive in the bar three months ago. The executive, who is married and has a family, became his lover for a while. They would meet on Friday afternoons and stay together until the next day. But the insurance executive failed to show up one Friday, and Paul never saw him again.

Paul was once beaten up by a man who made an advance to him but called him a "dirty faggot" when they were alone. He took Paul's billfold. And Paul was arrested inside a park by a cop who first made an advance, then took him in on a charge of soliciting.

Paul is pouring a cup of coffee for a customer in the hamburger joint. He doesn't know where to go or what to do with his life. It seems to be moving away from him very fast.

Mrs. DOUGLASS IS SITTING IN A CHAIR TRYING TO THINK. Her roommate has turned the TV set very loud, and this makes concentration on any thought or idea difficult. The room in the rest home is antiseptically clean and very, very white. It has two beds and two dressers. Now a nurse is walking through the door of the room.

Mrs. Douglass has five pictures and a calendar on the wall above her bed. One picture is of her son Will who died in 1944 in the war. Another is of her daughter Joan. It was taken at Joan's wedding forty years ago. The remaining pictures are of Joan's three children. These grandchild photographs are baby ones. The calendar has a nice painting of a forest on it. Beneath Mrs. Douglass's bed is a cardboard box containing the poems she used to write about the flowers in her garden at home.

Joan, who lives eighteen miles away, will be coming in to see Mrs. Douglass today. It is one of her three visits each week and she'll stay half an hour, bringing along friends' letters of interest and a new book or magazine. Next October Mrs.

Douglass will be eighty-one. She has lived in the rest home for the last eight years.

Mrs. Douglass looks at the calendar on the wall, not seeing it. She remembers her home. Her mind is far away.

THE OLD MAN IS SELLING NEWSPAPERS ON THE STREET.
"Evening paper," he calls out on his corner. "Buy it here." He has seen all the headlines and hawked all the stories. War Spreads to Cambodia! Earthquake in California! Nixon Wins! Moon Landing! Riot in Detroit! Marilyn Monroe Dead! Vietnam Massacre!

His eyes are runny. He is wearing an old gray sweater over his shirt and baggy pants. His familiar presence is as comforting to people as an old drugstore or a train terminal.

But he feels uneasy. His world has changed. He will tell you that he can remember when the city was genteel downtown. People were safe. There was law and order. The stores were fine. Only the best people went into the grand restaurants. The hotels were like palaces.

If you buy him a beer, he'll tell you that now he is baffled by the people he sees on the streets. "They're hippies and niggers and white trash," he'll say. "I'd kill my daughter if she went out with any of them. Kill her."

A fire engine with clanging bells roars by, charging up the street. The old man smiles. "Evening paper," he calls in a clear voice. "Buy it here."

Emily is sitting behind the plate glass window.

She doesn't really have to work. It's always been nice to know that. But Emily enjoys working. She has been employed for many years by the bank and is now an assistant manager.

The kids grew up all right without having her around the house. Harry has his own life at his store, she has hers at the bank, and they converge at the dinner table with the TV evening news.

She likes the cool serenity of Boon Savings with its cultivated conversational tone, brisk flow of human traffic, modern decor, underlying formality, and a tacit awareness that inside these doors warmth must always be chilled with just the right dash of impersonality.

It has occurred to Emily that the bank serves many of the purposes that a medieval cathedral did. Here is a cool sanctuary from the heated round of life outside. One can count upon firm dogma and a ritual of predictable behavior. There is absolute assurance of a remote salvation.

Emily stands up to shake hands with a client. Her face breaks into a businesslike and reserved warm smile. The Lover smiles back at her.

GINNY IS IN THE SUPERMARKET.

She finds the colors of apple juice, tomato juice, and prune juice to be like sophisticated stripes in a high fashion dress. The wrappings around dinner napkins, toilet tissue, and paper towels for the kitchen remind her of the upholstery in a cool, chic summer house overlooking a nice bay somewhere.

The spices are in small bottles whose style is stimulating to Ginny. She can have these little signs even if she can't own what they indicate to her.

Over there on a rack are the magazines with stories about celebrities. She wants to buy a few of these.

Ginny needs to buy a new container of oregano. Perhaps she'll pick up oyster stew for her lunch. Some French bread would be nice, too.

Ginny always hoped she would find the perfect romance, but the odds were against it. Her marriage has become something that she walks through. At least the days are free and hers alone. At night she observes the pragmatic plainness of a man who is simply and unmistakably not the prince with whom she could communicate at every level of her being. She is moving her food cart up the frozen food aisle of the supermarket.

MELVIN IS STARVING TO DEATH.

He is six months old. A lot of things have ganged up against him—population explosion, poverty, the disruption of his family, and the colossal indifference of nearly everybody to his life and death.

He is alternately ignored and beaten. His aged and helpless grandmother, half-seeing him through virtually blind eyes, believes fervently that his soul will simply fly away from the body when he dies and commence another cycle of life. Meanwhile, Melvin is crying softly. Thirst and hunger, neglect and abuse, are obliterating his feel for life. Death is raging in his bones, blood, and consciousness, claiming them.

The Lover claims him.

Bob is about to have lunch.

Standing outside a fashionable restaurant, he waits for two business clients. They will talk over a large real estate loan.

He attracts glances from people, for he is handsome in his smart new suit with a striped tie. He conveys an impression of strength and virility.

Inside, Bob will sit with his clients in a dimly lit room with bronze ornaments, immaculate white tablecloths, uniformed waiters taking orders for drinks before lunch, an aura of hard success, and the most expensive menu in town.

Still standing out on the street, however, Bob reveals a sober frown on his face. He is worried about the bite that taxes took out of his income, his son's involvement in drugs, what his wife's therapist told her last Tuesday, the immediate need to have new roofing placed on their house, and the doctor's report suggesting that his cholesterol is too high.

He would like to sort everything out and come up with answers. Yet he doesn't think there is time right now.

HE IS A THIRTY-SEVEN-YEAR-OLD SHOESHINE BOY.

Hank is black. He works in a shack that stands next door to a parking lot.

A man dressed in a business suit and carrying a briefcase has stopped in for a shine.

Hank soaps the shoes first. Then he uses his fingers and hands to apply black polish to them. Now he carefully rubs in the polish, massaging the shoes. His head, topped with graying short hair, is bent low over the customer's feet. Hank wears a smock. His brown jacket is hung on a nail on the wall of the shoeshine shack.

He is too busy to observe the people walking by: an Italian mother and her daughter on their way to visit a department store, a black student who plays basketball in high school, a white junior executive hurrying to a meeting.

Hank makes the customer's shoes shine with a white cloth. Now he takes another cloth to finish polishing the shoes with quick, firm strokes. He dips a small brush into a jar of black liquid polish, then tidily runs it around the sides of the shoes.

He stands up straight and says, "Thank you, sir." His customer puts down a newspaper he has been reading, gives Hank fifty cents, and walks out.

Now Hank climbs up in the chair and sits there quietly. He looks out at the street. The people walking by don't see him. The Lover does.

A MANNEQUIN SMILES INSIDE THE DEPARTMENT STORE WINDOW.

A revolving door leads into that special world. It is a city by itself. It has a post office, a larger population than many towns, a fleet of trucks, two restaurants, miles of departments, shelves of books, more jewelry than Topkapi, and enough suits for an army.

Mrs. Roberts comes into view.

She wears a small, proper-looking hat and gloves, along with her favorite dress. Having made a purchase in the store, she carries a small shopping bag bearing the store's well-known, exclusive imprint.

The shopping bag will receive glances when Mrs. Roberts climbs aboard the number 34 bus for the ride back to her small apartment on the west side. She has lived there alone during these nine years since her husband died. He left enough insurance so that she can get by if she is extremely careful. But dollars and cents are always going out, never coming in. This makes her feel anxious.

One day each week Mrs. Roberts dresses up for her visit to the department store downtown. It is the ageless home that she believes will never be taken away from her. Its elegance is bracing, evoking a flood of happy memories. Its familiarity has become an expression for her of communicated love.

Mrs. Roberts, carrying her shopping bag, walks toward me.

Sʜᴇ ɪs ᴡᴀʟᴋɪɴɢ ᴜᴘ ᴛʜᴇ sᴛʀᴇᴇᴛ.

Jeanne's blond hair doesn't look pretty anymore. Nervousness shows in her body movements and eyes.

Now she has stopped to look at a white wedding gown in a store window. She remembers how her wedding was a socially prominent one. However, soon afterwards when Jeanne realized that she was a stranger to herself, she fled.

Jeanne arrived in the city a month ago, after she had left her husband and baby. She stays in a hotel.

Her loneliness seems unbearable. She tries to obliterate it inside the hotel bar, a dingy place with dim lights and the barest suggestion of an oriental motif. Jeanne comes in around ten o'clock in the morning for a whisky sour. If she meets a man whom she likes, she takes him up to her room.

She's back in the bar at noon. Maybe there's another man whom she meets. Jeanne likes sex, but she also desires the tenderness of being held by a man's warm body inside the private world that is a bed. It seems nice that the man remains anonymous. He will not be able to make a lot of complicated demands.

She believes that she should really return home to pick up the pieces of her life. Yet she decides to wait at least until the end of the week, or maybe the start of next week.

She needs The Lover and the experience of loving and being loved.

H<small>E SAW ME LOOKING AT HIM.</small>

So he put on his mask right away. He is locked into his role. His is a mask designed to shield vulnerability. His vulnerability is simply his humanness; he has never known what to do with that. It has seemed easier to be a predictable machine that functions in every kind of human weather, under all possible circumstances and all sorts of crises, with efficiency and impersonality.

It angers him that other men of his age have had fathers supporting them through four or more years of life on a campus. He did not have a father to do that. His father disappeared a long time ago, leaving his mother and himself to manage as best they could. Now he is twenty-three. After going to night school for several years, he finally won his college degree.

He feels acutely that because he had to work hard for everything, he does not want to share it with anyone. He asks: Why should feelings ever get in the way of advancement that offers the only escape from drudgery?

He dresses for warmth in the winter, comfort in the summer, and a proper image. He says that he cannot bask in the luxury of individual expression, something designed for dilettantes or people who had security handed to them on a silver platter.

But he worries that his mask may not always allow breathing space.

Mary ellen just received a telephone call.

It was from a guy whom she's been dating. He also is on drugs as she is.

She says that it is easier to go out with somebody who understands because he has the same problem. She feels inadequate and defensive, she explains, with a nice guy. Then there's some kind of standard to come up to that makes her feel helpless and cheap.

Mary Ellen has served time in the women's prison. She once got into prostitution to raise money for drugs. Now she is on probation and hopes that her continued use of drugs won't show up in the tests they give her.

Well, her plans are all set for tonight. She's drinking another cup of coffee and glancing at the morning paper. Her mom just asked who called her.

Mary Ellen knows that she needs help but won't ask for it. A sense of futility gnaws at her because she feels that she is slipping off of a cliff. The Lover would like to come into her life and bring her hope. Will Mary Ellen let him come in?

Mʀ. ᴀɴᴅ ᴍʀs. ᴄᴀʀʟᴇᴛᴏɴ sᴍɪᴛʜ ᴀʀᴇ sᴇᴀᴛᴇᴅ ɪɴ ᴛʜᴇ ᴅᴏᴄ-
ᴛᴏʀ's ʀᴇᴄᴇᴘᴛɪᴏɴ ʀᴏᴏᴍ.

Mr. Smith is ordinarily at the office by this
time of morning, so he glances involuntarily toward the hands of an electric clock on the wall.
Minutes hang heavily in the room where already
nine people are seated while waiting to see various doctors. He picks up a six-month-old copy of
the *National Geographic,* absently looking at
color photographs of Copenhagen.

Mrs. Smith hopes it is benign. After the doctor
removes the keratoacanthoma growth from her
hand this morning, the necessary tests will require
ten days. The verrucaid keratosis on her back
proved, thank God, to be benign. Yet she reminds
herself that the keratosis on her upper lip was not
benign and all too threatening. Then she had to
take x-ray therapy.

Now she picks up an ancient copy of *News-
week* from a pile of magazines. The cover story is
about her favorite author. She replaces the magazine and glances around the room at the other
people who are waiting. There is a high-school
student slumped in his chair apparently sleeping,
a nervous young couple, an old man, a businessman with a pipe, a woman who must be a school

teacher. The Lover looks at her. She feels that she cannot stand more of this waiting. Does she have cancer? Is she going to die? "Mrs. Smith," a blond nurse wearing a crisp white uniform announces from the door.

Mr. and Mrs. Carleton Smith stand up.

V

Some people simply build high walls around their own lives.

Other people spend years inside a prison maintained by society to confine them. The lover moved through prison walls with me.

Living hell is laid against the instinct of a man."

The thirty-one-year-old inmate spoke with bitterness. He had served twelve years behind bars.

"My youth and life have been used up," he said. "They're always taking more away from you than you ever took away from society. You're so alone."

I started to say something, but he rode over my words. "The only corrective force in the world is the goodness and kindness that opens up life. Until you can link yourself again to the instinctual force that loves, you are lost. Love is the only corrective thing in the world. I've lain on my bunk and just wished that I could die. For what it costs to keep a man in prison, they could give a man a new and positive start."

His face had deep lines set in it.

"I try to keep my mind and spirit on nature. I watch birds, one chasing another. It's more of a show. Their anger is done in mockery and in the moment. There's no hangover like humans have, where something is done and twenty years later it is still being dealt with."

His passion ran through the sieve of my listening.

I'VE LEARNED MORE CRIME IN HERE, MAN."

A young inmate and I were talking in the prison yard. He had a scar above his left eye.

"I didn't consider myself a hardened criminal at seventeen when I came in here," he said. "But I've learned the ropes of a hardened criminal in here, dig? There have been times when it was a regular occurrence to see somebody come up the hall bleeding. On the streets I wouldn't want to see anybody dead. But here in the joint I've learned to be more sadistic."

His eyes were nervous and sad, but my attention was distracted from them when his face broke into a hard smile.

"I don't think locking up a man is curing anything. But I know there has to be something done, dig?, to keep people in line. Some discipline. Yet for me to learn more crime here than I ever knew on the street is not cool at all. You put a person in a cage. To say it is rehabilitation is not cool at all, man."

He sat before me with a presence that seemed to grow. His eyes hungrily searched my face.

As I get older I get more nervous."

He was nearly sixty years old and had been in prison for a decade. His whiteness was chalk-like, his face puffy.

"I'm getting to the point where I want everything uncomplicated. When you plan a little here, and a little there, it gets complicated. I just want to be honest and above-board without complications."

He shrugged his shoulders gently.

"But in here you'd be dead if you did that. Or you'd find there'd be someone walking ahead of you in the food line who'd take your dessert. You've got to have a chip on your shoulder. Everybody's your judge. Anybody can go get your jacket—your record. They say, 'I'll get even with him for society.' They won't let you be a person."

He sat uneasily in his chair, looking down at his hands resting on his knees.

"I was a loser once before, I am what my environment is. If I live around good people, I become a good person. If I live in a lousy situation, I'm a lousy person. You're all thrown together here and you are who you're with, that's all. You're losing before you start. Being here isn't conducive to being anything but lost."

We sat with The Lover in the growing silence.

THE TRAGEDY IN HERE IS THAT YOU FORGET YOUR DAY-BY-DAY EXISTENCE."

Of his last thirty years, twenty-eight have been spent in prison. He is in his fifties. Once he was a mechanic.

"I was out on parole for over a year in 1946. And for a while in 1948.

"Time doesn't exist any more. What does exist is that you know you're in prison. The mechanism just blanks out the years. To think of twenty-eight years, you know, could drive you crazy."

He brushed this aside. Leaning close to me, he spoke animatedly, "I had a very interesting experience. I got to go home once for just part of a day. Home felt the same as it always had before. And when I was there I felt that the prison never existed. But, you know, when I got back to prison that night, it was as if the world of my home had never existed. I'd never been there."

Iᴛ ʜᴀꜱɴ'ᴛ ᴅᴏɴᴇ ᴀɴʏᴛʜɪɴɢ ꜰᴏʀ ᴍᴇ. ʙᴜᴛ ɪᴛ'ꜱ ᴅᴏɴᴇ ᴀ ʟᴏᴛ ᴛᴏ ᴍᴇ."

He is fifty years old and has been a prisoner for the past twenty.

"There's nothing normal about prison the way they have it now. If you have a friend who's an inmate, you always know a time will come when the friendship will end. The law says it has to end. You're really not supposed to communicate with the next inmate. Even if you made friends with staff, you couldn't see them outside because they're not supposed to associate with ex-inmates."

He turned his face away from me as he spoke, averting my gaze. His words were sometimes almost unintelligible for he did not raise his voice to be heard.

"I've spent more of my adult years in prison than outside. I was a victim of my immaturity and wouldn't let anybody help me. But is this a reason to keep anybody in prison for twenty years? I'm kind of angry sometimes. I ask how could I be so stupid and weak to get myself into this shape."

Y<small>OU FEEL MAD.</small>"

A prisoner who was forty-four years old sat across from me.

"You feel disgusted. Then you get mad at yourself for feeling disgusted. You get in bed and pull the covers over your head and try to mentally change the subject."

He gestured impatiently with his hands.

"How would you feel if you were being made into a homosexual and there was nothing on earth you could do to stop it?

"You go out into the yard. The talk there is about Mao or Che. Or somebody says socialism is better than capitalism. You can talk about one of a thousand things. What difference does it make?"

He made a gesture of futility, dropping his hands.

"You have a woman visitor. But you're told that you're too close to her. You're holding hands and you shouldn't do that. You're kissing too long."

He stretched his body. "How can you explain how not to be killed by a system and then left to die?"

THEY NEVER TELL YOU ANYTHING."

He had been behind bars since 1948 except once when he was out on parole for thirty-three months.

"Somebody told me in 1970 that the psychology and aptitude tests I took in 1948 all came out art. If I'd known this when they processed me, there's a real possibility my whole life all these years could have been different.

"The point is, since I've started painting, I've got a lot better insight into my life. I feel free. I feel that I can see the truth. The truth is that I don't need anything. I can live without anything. The high life out there. I don't have to go out there and pull those robberies and drink that booze and run over the country like I did."

He looked older than his forty-seven years. I saw an elderly man dressed in regulation denim shirt and pants, bearing a number that had replaced his name. Whom did The Lover see?

Survival comes ahead of getting out."

An inmate in his twenties was speaking. He looked at me coolly, talking softly.

"You fear for your life. If you get killed or rot while you're here, it won't do you any good thinking about getting out. First you've got to make it here, man. Survival can come down to what it's all about."

I wondered who his parents, companions, relatives, and friends were on the outside in that other part of his life.

"You know, you can go days and months without your mind ever leaving the institution. It becomes an effort to even think about anything not associated with the prison. In a lot of cases, strange as it may seem, black inmates aren't aware of 85 percent of what's going on in the black community outside."

His face expressed neither boredom nor surprise, humor nor sadness.

"There's a lot of prison outside too. People settle back and get married and have a family and move around in a thirty-five-mile radius. They confine themselves. They don't know 85 percent of what's going on in the community either."

He looked around us at his present world of guards, inmates, monotony, rules, uniforms, guns, and locked doors.

To be in prison is to be black, period."

He was in his early thirties and had been behind bars most of his adult life.

"North America is the prison. Anytime you have anybody control your destiny, you're locked up. Black in the system means the last hired, the first fired. What does black mean in a sick twisted society? What is there to get out of? It's hard to realize what is reality and fantasy.

"You breathe clean air. You take for granted the good I think we are all likely to have in us. But where does my prison end? It started thirty-two years ago when I was born. My prison will probably last until there is total, absolute racial separation or total, absolute annihilation of one of the races."

He had a scar on his face and a front tooth had been chipped. Hard lines had settled into his black face. His Afro hair was streaked with white strands. His eyes smoldered, yet possessed kindness.

"We're 10 percent of the population outside but 45 percent of the population in here. I want to know what segment of society tells me I have to be placed here. Did the good people do this? Black people are stuck off in holes and forgotten. Black people are slaughtered for no reason at all."

He paused and we sat together in silence. When he resumed speaking, his voice was so low that I could scarcely hear it. Only then did I notice that tears stood in his eyes.

"When I first came to prison the average age was twenty-eight. Now it's twenty-two or twenty-three—and black. I think it's genocide against my people. But that isn't just in prison. America is committing genocide against my people. What hurts is that there's nothing I can do about it. How can a man be dead and define his feelings?"

E VERY MAN MUST WRITE HIS OWN POEM."

The young inmate had a worn, exhausted face. He was a highly sensitive man, an intellectual cut off from immediate hope for his development as a person.

"To write your own poem is to show the strength of your inner dream," he told me.

His eyes withdrew, recollecting an event that I could not share.

"I had my whole world destroyed before my eyes. I went into an emotional shock thing that brought deep disturbances and torments and agonies. The whole world as I saw it, dreamed of it, and hoped for it was destroyed."

He remained absorbed in a shroud of silence that felt bitter cold and menacing.

"The death wish thing comes when people running a prison like this try to kill life. Inmates are returned to a condition like infancy but are supposed to adjust to the world as it is. So a man either moves into real bitterness or else accepts apathy. Most choose apathy. You could call it our way of life."

The color gray seemed to permeate one's senses, drowning reds, yellows, and blues. Life was choreographed but only very narrowly, tightly, even strait-jacketed in a closed society. Yet The Lover was inside as well as outside the prison walls.

The time passed.

VI

THE LOVER HAS BEEN PRESENT WITH ME IN COMPLEX
AND DEMANDING SITUATIONS, RAISING SHARP
QUESTIONS IN MY MIND AND REMINDING ME HOW
I NEEDED HUMILITY AND COMPASSION ABOVE ALL.

WE MAY HAVE 100 YEARS REMAINING OF HUMAN LIFE," HE SAID.

The scientist and I were having lunch beneath colorful coats-of-arms inside the quiet confines of a private club.

"The moon shot will go down in history as the high point of what Western civilization was able to accomplish," he said. "From now on everything will be regression."

He lit a cigarette.

"You see, we made too many mistakes. I suppose our progress was too swift, without adequate introspection or weighing of values. Now we can't turn back to correct these certain things.

"Oh, there might still be a few years—perhaps ten—to reverse the tide against us. But we're not doing anything significant about it. Our best scientists are merely patronized as Cassandras. People hear the sounds of warning but cannot bring themselves to listen. I'm not at all optimistic."

Did I want beefsteak or rare prime ribs for lunch? the waiter who came to our table asked. Had he heard the words of the scientist or only the sounds? His eyes expressed no alarm.

"It's a pity we couldn't have got to outer space earlier," the scientist continued. "Man in a later period will surely manage to do it. You see, I am saying that human life will somehow survive on earth. But only a small residue of it in a most primitive form. It will take uncanny planning combined with luck even for that. If it can survive, the species will fight its way back to dominance again. Next time I hope it will learn from its past mistakes."

The waiter poured our coffee in porcelain cups. The level of conversation around us was subdued, broken into occasionally by a man's sudden laughter or a greeting called to a friend across several tables.

"There is a serious role for religion in these next few years," the scientist said. "As life winds down and the quality of it disintegrates, religion can prepare people for a gentle death instead of a hard one. No bitterness. No hate. No anger about human fate."

Did I want cheesecake, a napoleon, or ice cream for dessert?

"In the face of mass death there can emerge a reverence for life that is altogether new," the scientist told me. "People can enjoy life and each other and the universe. Maybe people can become really human in these last years of civilization."

Finally we stood up to go, making our way

past tables of guests toward the cloak room. In a hallway I held him back for a moment by placing my hand on his arm. He stopped and turned around to face me.

"Do you really believe this?" I asked.

His eyes were both deadly serious and extremely kind, with sadness stalking them.

"Yes," he replied.

We walked outside the club into the city air, parting to go our separate ways. I wandered up the street, noticing people's faces, and, amid the furious pace of life, I saw The Lover.

I SEEMED TO BE IN A FILM BUT WAS NOT DIRECTING IT.
Angry voices were shouting. There were threats of bodily harm. Someone laughed in a shrill, loud voice bordering on hysteria. The flashing red lights of police cars framed the scene.

I was standing in line with sixty black students who sought admission to a segregated movie theater in a small southern college town. The students refused to buy tickets for the "Negro section" in the balcony, demanding entrance to whatever seats they wished to occupy. The theater manager refused. The police had been called.

Angry white townspeople hurried to the theater. They demanded that the students be placed under arrest. The people surrounded the students, calling out at them with racial insults and harsh threats. The men and women students, frightened by the show of power against them, maintained an uneasy but outward calm.

I wondered once again what things inside a person's imagination or feelings explode to produce this kind of hatred. Did the townspeople think the students' original sin was their blackness? If so, who had taught them that?

My whiteness burned me as I sought my humanness with The Lover in the central and intimate places beneath color, sex, nationality, rank, or name.

N<small>O WHITE MAN IS REALLY FREE,"</small> THE BLACK PSYCHI-
<small>ATRIST TOLD ME.</small>

A fire crackled in the grate of his study as we talked. He was a lean, wiry man, dressed casually in a knit sports shirt and wool slacks.

"I'm aware that black people have to change themselves from psychological bonds imposed by society," he continued. "But that alone will not bring about the kind of freedom needed in this country. As I see it, the white man needs freeing if the black man is to be free. If a white man tends to enslave anyone else, psychologically or through institutional racism, then he is also enslaved."

The black psychiatrist spoke easily but his eyes flashed.

"Whites' image of themselves is as distorted as the black self-image. White people think of themselves as superior when they are only equal. Only a few whites who have the money, power, or prestige are able to act out their superiority successfully. The others are repressed but may not know it. So whites need to see themselves as they really are. Then they can see other people as they are."

He continued reflectively. "Any thinking black

man must be aware of at least two levels of consciousness. First, the fulfillment of his blackness—that is to say, his freedom as a man. Second, knowing how to operate in a society whose value system is somehow both corrupt and inviting.

"So blacks have to be suspicious. This sounds pathological, but I maintain that it is a normal defensive mechanism. Black paranoia is almost necessary in order to survive."

Remaining quiet for a few moments, he then said, "The black achieving person, such as myself, who is increasingly exposed to problems of his society beyond himself, has a special task. He must be perpetually involved in the problem that the poor black, while perhaps free in spirit, remains horribly deprived. I am always working to change that situation."

COLORED TILES COVERED THE CATHEDRAL FLOOR.
They were turquoise, rose, bright green, olive, brown, and yellow. My feet rested on them. I wondered: How many feet have shuffled over these tiles toward the altar to receive the bread of life? How many feet have rested on these tiles in prayer? How many feet have marched up the center aisle of the cathedral in a wedding procession, an ordination to the holy ministry, or a final human parting with a loved one in a funeral service here? The colors of the tiles were faded.

I thought of the original religious movement that gave birth to cathedrals. People were on fire with love for God and other people. When did the movement become a gigantic organization? Rules eroded loving. Outsiders came to be considered outsiders. Comfortable words replaced uncomfortable ones. Prophets became scarce. Prayer turned into rote.

I asked The Lover: Can religion become a successful, big organization without losing its soul?

I RESTED IN A PEW INSIDE THE CATHEDRAL.

A prayer book lay beside me. I opened the book and turned its pages. There were dozens of prayers for all occasions. One was for a marriage ceremony. Another was a petition for inner strength.

I asked: Can prayer be a thought, a smile, a tear, a glance, or an action as well as a word? Then I closed the prayer book, placed it inside a wooden rack and sat quietly inside the cathedral with The Lover.

Winding stairs led up to the cathedral pulpit.

I wondered if the preacher were young, middle-aged or old. Did he still feel hope or had he lost it? Did he love people? Did he court easy popularity or was he secure enough within himself to speak and live the truth as he saw it?

Yes, I knew that it would be very hard to stand inside that pulpit and speak the truth. Most people did not really want to hear it. Much of established religion has generally tended to be very quiet when it should have been witnessing, patiently and outspokenly, for God's Word over against the tragedies of war and man's always localized and highly specific inhumanity to man.

The nation's flag stood inside the cathedral sanctuary. It made me think of the tragedy which occurs when religion is on too easy terms with any government. Then the church often becomes a kind of department, or compartment, of religion within the state. It does not criticize wrong government decisions, question the ambiguous motives of politicians, or speak out against outrages committed by the state.

I hoped that the sermons inside the cathedral were truthful, loving and brave ones.

A MAN KNELT AT THE BACK OF THE CATHEDRAL.

He held his bowed head in his hands. His frayed shirt, dirty pants and mud-caked shoes stood in curious contrast with the white marble altar, golden candlesticks, and priceless stained glass.

I asked myself if I should interrupt the man, greet him as a brother, and offer him assistance, food, money, clothing, or simply my time in order to listen.

Was The Lover this man?

A<small>N UNCONTROLLABLE CRY FORCED ITSELF INTO MY</small>
T<small>HROAT.</small>

The poverty which I saw around me on the lonely Indian reservation was like an open sore. The people felt helpless to bring about any kind of change in their lives. The homes of these people were miserable shacks. There was insufficient food and heat.

I talked with Indian men inside the jail. They had left the reservation in order to seek a better life in a city and a decent chance to succeed. Lacking adequate training and help, they had failed. Upon returning here, they had sought deep solace in the suicidal forgetfulness of liquor. Now locked inside a jail cell, they saw hope diminish even farther away.

These were not costumed figures in a museum or strange characters in a Hollywood western film. They were living men and women seeking to discover the presence of The Lover in acts of love offered to them by other men and women in their society.

I AM ON THE EDGE OF MADNESS," HE TOLD ME.

He was a graduate student at the university, an ex-G.I. back home after fighting in Vietnam. He spoke quietly, drinking beer, but occasionally his voice rose against the crescendo of the loud recorded music.

We sat together in Mr. Iron's, a student hangout. The time was past midnight. The jukebox played "Around the World."

"Gravity is pulling me down," the student said. "I don't know whether to go on with law or seriously try to become a writer. What is pure law? What is pure art? I have a highly subjective point of view about things now."

The jukebox was turned off as Mr. Iron, the proprietor, sat down at an ancient piano to play "As Time Goes By."

"To what extent does a highly subjective point of view contaminate art or corrupt law?" the student asked. "I've seen blood. There are men I knew who are dead. Are *they* objective? How can I be? But I'm told that my present feeling gets in the way of objectivity. I don't have patience right now. I don't know what to do with my strong feelings."

The Lover had joined us, listening.

A TELEVISION CREW VISITED THE MONASTERY.

The TV producer, worried about his program's sagging ratings felt it was a fresh new angle for a ten minute time slot. The prior of the monastery believed that the national publicity could help evangelize the nation, assist fund raising efforts, and possibly bring in a few badly needed new recruits as novices.

On the day when the TV crew visited the monastery there was a sharing of chaos for everybody. The monks could not pray on schedule because they were kept busy rehearsing various scenes before shooting them. The TV crew had to haul equipment inside the tiny Romanesque chapel, wire it for sound, and set up lights.

The mass needed to be simulated for filming. So did the ceremony of a monk's taking his life vows. The sacred words were halted again and again by shouted instructions from the TV director to the monks, instructing them to change positions, to kneel facing a camera for a close-up, or sometimes to pray more loudly.

Tempers became frayed as the monks felt divine ground was being trod upon by hard secularists, and the TV staff abhorred the monks' sheltered life that seemed not to complement the rhythms of the complex life they knew in the world.

Finally the work was completed, five hours late. Everybody was exhausted. Driving away, the TV producer sped along a country road toward the city in his Porsche. He contemplated a hot shower and a cold martini. Back in the monastery, the prior pondered the theology of modern culture and asked himself if this momentary absorption in secular involvement was really worth the alleged benefits.

Why couldn't the monks and the TV crew relate to The Lover and to each other as human beings?

A LOT OF BLACKS ARE STILL FILLED WITH SELF-HATRED," THE BLACK EDUCATOR SAID.

"Generally we've stopped buying ointment to lighten our skin," he continued. "However, we're too often still trying to whiten the mind. The more that blackness becomes vogue with blacks, the faster we're going to hip ourselves into being black."

He stood up and walked around the room as he talked to me.

"You see, I have to accept the fact that there was slavery in my family. It was there. I can't get hung up about it in the task of getting myself together. Once I say I was a slave, I know how far I have to go in order to be a man.

"Then I laugh about it. For it is unthinkable that I could ever be a slave today. I have done something to my mind so that the alternatives would now be unmistakably freedom or death."

The black educator showed me photographs of his two young sons.

"I am not just their father," he said. "I am their ancestry. I must make visible a new, free life style to them. To blacken the mind is to come back and accept what has happened historically and then restructure it in terms of self-acceptance."

I SAW THE CRIPPLED WOMAN.

Propelling her body from a reservoir of internal energy, she attempted to cross the busy street corner. It required superhuman strength to place one foot before the other, moving resolutely in front of idling cars which were momentarily halted by a red light.

The drivers inside the cars displayed impatience at the sign of her presence. Would she manage to cross the street before the traffic light turned to green? They watched her movements in an unfriendly atmosphere of curiosity, disgust, and pity.

She had got half of the way through her difficult passage. Her face revealed tension, impatience, and fear. The traffic light changed. A horn sounded. Her twisted body slowly, determinedly moved ahead. But then she relaxed and her face broke into a smile. The Lover was laughing with her.

GUSTS OF WIND BLEW THROUGH CANYONS OF STEEL IN THE CITY AT NIGHT.

It was lonely standing on the dark street surrounded by skyscrapers whose lights were suspended high above the ground. An old man, his coat collar turned up as protection against the cold night air, was my sole companion on the street as he peered through a hole in the wooden fence surrounding the building site.

An entire city block had been leveled to make room for the new building. Men had knocked down an old residential hotel, two dozen shops, a lunch counter, an Italian restaurant, a music store, a bookstore, and an office building. One block away stood another building whose peak seemed to scrape the sky.

I felt very small and unconnected and was grateful that The Lover is in the city.

I'VE ARRIVED AT THE POINT WHERE I NO LONGER WANT TO HELP ANYBODY," HE SAID.

The middle-aged, white Protestant minister and I were engaged in conversation. He had long been a leader in the peace movement and civil rights within his community.

"I want out of the business of being the supreme leader," he told me. "I don't want to create any dependency upon me. I don't want to help my wife or children. I don't want to help poor people. Helping people seems to create all over again the supremacy clause."

We talked inside the living room of his home where he had shed shoes and socks. He was dressed in a soiled T-shirt and work pants.

"I'm going to work for the Third World, the world's oppressed and disenfranchised, by attempting to organize poor people here in our city," he said. "I feel existing political structures can be changed by nonviolent, long-range action. I see a ten year struggle ahead."

I asked him about his feelings as a white man working with black men and women.

"Integration and separatism are non-words to me," he said. "We can't stand on blackness and whiteness at this point. I'm no longer going to put it down on being white."

He chose his words with care, speaking softly.

"I have been in situations where human help was needed. My concern for the black image to assert itself was knocked in the head. Nobody black could do it. The truth was just that I had more skill than anybody else there. The whole situation crossed any color line.

"Another human being was in trouble. I had at my fingertips the knowledge. I helped."

The white Protestant minister paused.

"But I don't like that word. Let's say I did what I could."

VII

THE LOVER LET ME PERCEIVE THE ANXIETY AND SHARE
THE PAIN OF JIM, A YOUNG MAN, AND CAROL, A YOUNG
WOMAN.

> THE LOVER CONFRONTED ME WITH THE CHALLENGE
> OF TRYING TO MEET THEIR NEED OF UNDERSTAND-
> ING, EVEN WHILE ANY KIND OF TOTAL ANSWER TO
> THEIR PROBLEM ELUDED ME. MANY PEOPLE WOULD
> ASK: DID JUDGMENT EXCLUDE FORGIVENESS? THE
> LOVER OPENED UP MY FEELINGS TO COMPREHEND
> THE COMPELLING NEED OF FORGIVENESS SO THAT
> HEALING COULD TOUCH ALL OF THE LIVES CAUGHT
> IN THE DEPTHS OF THIS TRAGEDY.

J<small>IM</small>:

Soul. I guess I don't have it.

Do only blacks have soul?

I was never free, I guess. I won't ever be free.
I'll be dead. Maybe dead is free.

I forgot to get my shirts and pants at the cleaner's. Better do that first thing Monday.

Have I got a clean shirt for tomorrow?

Wednesday is the day.

Wednesday.

CAROL:

Daddy isn't home.

He's in Chicago, mom said.

Why does he want to make more money?

Please, daddy, come home, please, daddy, come
home.

The moon is full.

Is there a man in the moon or is it mountains?

Wednesday.

What will I do after Wednesday?

The moon is so full.

Jᴵᴹ:

Carol, I love you.
I love you, Carol.
Who can I believe about anything?
Carol, I don't know what to do, baby.
    I really don't know what to do, Carol.

C_{AROL}:

Jim, when you loved me.
Jim, you made me so happy.
I never knew I could be that happy.
You're so beautiful, Jim.

It takes my breath away when I look at you.
I could die just being with you.
I forget everything else when I'm with you, Jim.
I'm so scared. There's no time and you're not here.
Jim, I think I want to die.
I'm scared tonight. I'm afraid of Wednesday.

JIM:

Why can't I call you, Carol?

I'm scared. I'm so tired I could die.

Carol, we can't have a life together. On Wednesday they have called me to go away to war.

There isn't any life except our baby's. It is growing inside you, Carol.

The baby is three months old inside you.

I won't marry you before I go away, Carol. I love you but I can't. I'm lost and confused. I didn't want a baby. I didn't plan on a baby. I'm not ready to be a father, Carol, or a husband.

Carol, I'm still a kid. I'm a boy. I don't know life yet. I want to know life, Carol, but all they're going to let me know is death.

Help me, Carol.

But it's you who needs help, isn't it? Carrying the baby. You haven't told your folks. I'm going away. We're not married.

I can't help you, Carol. There's no help left in me. I'm on thin, thin ice.

I love you, Carol.

C<small>AROL</small>:

    Yellow is the loveliest color.

    I would like to dress my baby in yellow.

    But I don't want my baby. I'm afraid to have my
        baby. (Why hasn't Jim called?)

    Wednesday is so near.

    Yes, I would choose yellow clothes for my baby.
        (What can I tell mom? Will daddy under-
        stand at all?)

    I like reds, too. And light blues. But yellows are
        so fresh and bright and hopeful.

Jim:

I want you, Carol.

I want to be with you. I want to hold you. I want to make love to you.

But there's no hope for us, Carol. I don't know what I'm doing. I don't know what they're doing to me.

I can't touch you. Either I'm going to kill people or they're going to kill me. Probably both. This is hopelessness. I don't want to kill anybody. I don't want to die.

My mom and dad expect me to go. They're proud of me, they say.

Why do they justify murder in war but not outside it?

Carol, I want you but can't come to you. I can't come to you this way.

CAROL:

I'll wait until after Jim goes away on Wednesday.

Then I'll tell my sister about the baby. I'll let her tell mom.

Mom will know the baby is Jim's, but I'll tell her I'm not sure.

I suppose they'll send me away some place to have the baby very quietly so no one will know. They'll expect me to let some married couple take my baby and make it theirs.

Jim, marry me. Please marry me, Jim, before Wednesday.

But I can't ask you. I won't ask you. I won't marry you unless you ask me to.

Mom will expect me to go to church with her to-morrow morning.

JIM:

If I could pray, I don't know what I'd ask for.
(Does praying mean asking for something?)
Okay. I'd ask for world peace. That should keep
God busy.
I wonder what world peace would be like.
It would probably wreck the economy.
What would the Chinese do if their armies were
disbanded? And the Russians? How many
men are in the Japanese, Portuguese, Indian,
French, and British armies?
If the Brazilian, Argentine, and Bolivian armies
were disbanded, how would jobs be found for
the soldiers?
World peace would throw everybody out of the
work of killing.

CAROL:

I remember Jean's wedding.

I was glad she asked me to be a bridesmaid.

It was so beautiful. Her gown took my breath away. The flowers were lovely.

Her father gave her away. Her mother looked so proud and happy.

When the priest said they were married, Larry kissed her right in front of the altar and everybody.

The music almost made me cry. But I guess it was a lot of other things too. Like the vows they made to each other. For richer, for poorer. In sickness or health. Until death.

Oh, Jim, I feel our baby inside me.

J<small>IM</small>:

When dad had his man-to-man talk with me, I
don't know which one of us was more em-
barrassed.

I knew everything he was telling me but couldn't
let on.

He told me about continence and patience, then
about condoms and the pill. He talked about
the first experience I would have with a
woman.

I tried to avoid looking him in the eyes. He
seemed to be staring at his shoes, but every
so often he would force himself to look right
at me and grab my shoulder.

Sex was good after marriage, he said.

He knew I'd have sex before marriage, but I
should try to control myself. If I couldn't, be
sure to use a condom. Or be sure the girl
used a pill. Or something—but don't make a
baby until a honeymoon.

We both knew it was a big joke, a big fraud, or
a real sad thing. Dad did the best he could,
but there was something phony about it.

Wednesday. Wednesday is almost here.

CAROL:

> Everybody is a whore, a poet said. But, the way people look at it, I'm really a whore. At least to them.
>
> If Jim would marry me, nobody would be shocked. Not even when the baby came early.
>
> Jim, I know how tormented you are. How scared you are. How under pressure you are until you can't breathe.
>
> I worried about you, Jim, yesterday when you were driving on the highway and I heard on the news that three people had died in an automobile crash just about where you were.
>
> But after Wednesday, when you go to war, will I have to worry all the time, Jim, or just try to forget?

JIM:

Why is death all I can see?

I see it on the TV news every night.

I see dead bodies. I see planes bombing. I see guys dying.

I feel sure I'll probably die there.

Nothing makes any sense to me.

Is this what civilization means? Then I think I don't want any part of it.

I didn't plan to make a baby to live in all this garbage. The baby happened. I didn't intend it. I can't claim it. I can't claim Carol as my wife. I love Carol. But I'm sick and touched by dying.

Can you understand, Carol?

I can't just tell you like out of a textbook, baby.

Do you understand?

C<small>AROL</small>:

Daddy married mom during a war.

Was mom pregnant before they got married?

Did mom think that daddy was going to get killed in the war?

They've never talked about it to me.

Mom has never told me how she felt about daddy.

I wish Jim and daddy could talk. But they can't.

I've seen mom's wedding pictures. She looked so pretty. She didn't look strained or unhappy at all.

I guess their generation was different.

Even though they had wars, they knew they couldn't blow up the world. The idea would never have occurred to them. So they had a kind of security.

We don't have any security at all, Jim and I, and the other kids.

JIM:

Sunday.

Monday.

Tuesday.

Wednesday.

Will it rain or will the sun be shining? I wonder if I'll even notice. But how will I remember the day?

What difference will it make?

Carol, you were so pretty in that yellow dress. You were smiling. You seemed happy. I loved you.

Carol, what is life about? What is our baby's life about?

Will our baby have to kill or be killed? Why?

I didn't want to make a baby who would have to kill or be killed.

Carol, forgive me.

CAROL:

I looked at a movie on television about the Second
World War.

I just don't understand why there can be war.

Do some people want war?

Do some people like to kill other people?

Do some people make a profit out of war?

If Jim dies, is there somebody who wants him to,
or profits from his death?

If not, why don't the leaders refuse to let there
be wars?

It seems to me that leaders should exist to serve
the people.

To serve the people means to watch out for their
best interests.

Can war ever be in the people's best interest?

Jim, Wednesday is so close.

Jɪᴍ:

Good-by, Carol.

I'm uptight and can't say anything.

I hope you understand.

Good luck with our kid. I guess your folks will
find a home for him.

I can't think ahead.

I don't know anything except that I am going to
war.

Also, I love you, Carol.

But now it's death before life.

So long, Carol.

CAROL:

I didn't notice when it started to rain.
I can hear it softly falling over my room.
Jim, I feel our baby.
Wednesday. Oh, Jim, Wednesday.
Yellow is such a nice, clean, bright color.
I would like to dress my baby in yellow.
Jim, good-by. Good-by, Jim.

VIII

I HAVE SHARED MANY QUESTIONS WITH THE LOVER, WHO
HAS BEEN A WITNESS TO MY CHANGING FEELINGS
AND VIEWS.

ZEALOTS SHOUTING "LOVE" WITH HATE IN THEIR EYES HAVE HORSEWHIPPED ME INTO THE ARMS OF GENTLENESS.

I get belly laughs from hard, humorless people whose macabre intensity rattles pictures in the hallway and scares the dog. I am chased headlong back into history by those who profess simply "now" as their alpha and omega.

Have various people and events rendered me perverse?

The explanation of the complex twistings of my behavior is that I seek self-determination. Buffeted by the winds of liberation movements, I smell freedom. I want some for myself. . . .

. . . . It seems to me this is not being selfish. Following a long study of wars inside and outside myself, I have learned that the fundamental prerequisite of any contribution I can make to world peace is the establishment of equilibrium at the center of my own life. I have found that the initial, essential way I can bring love to suffering, agonized, and loveless masses of humanity is to become a human being who freely gives and receives love.

Charisma, the electric light switch of cultic celebrity, sets my teeth on edge. Chic—whether it be conservative or liberal, moderate or radical—starts questions ticking in my mind. For co-optation is my mortal enemy.

"Things fall apart; the center cannot hold; mere anarchy is loosed upon the world . . ." I feel the strong flow of history around me. It seems necessary to achieve a sober and illuminating perspective about it. Only in this way can I survive and function creatively. The unhappy alternative is to become torn asunder by forces beyond my understanding or ability to discipline them. If mere anarchy is loosed upon the world, while the best lack all conviction and the worst are full of passionate intensity, and a rough beast, in one's mind or outside it, slouches toward Bethlehem, where shall the breach be held? . . .

. . . . The collective center comprises individual parts, including my own, that can be predicated on the resolute search for reality and nourishment of hope. Self-fulfilling prophecy of disaster is a psychotic specter. My essential task is, where at all possible, not to let things which may otherwise lie beyond my control fall apart in my own being and sphere of involvement. If the center holds within me, it holds somewhere in the human struggle. Self-determination and a commitment of solidarity with others are joined. The center holds somewhere in the universe.

I share fully in the personal anxiety that inevitably accompanies this moment in history with its seesaw rhythm of political action. *What do I want for myself in this moment?* . . .

. . . . I want to be an organic part of social responsibility and community building. Yet I also want to nurture my individuality—even if I must be called eccentric.

I want to weigh myself in the scales of liberation movements and hopefully increase human identity. Yet I do not want to live in a melting pot that denies deep and honest differences between people.

I want to be sufficiently sober and serious about the overwhelming questions of this day, this age: poverty, emptiness, ecology, identity, racism, loneliness in a mass, war. Yet I do not want to lose my sense of humor, capacity for sheer abandon, and awareness of the absurd as a quality of life. . . .

. . . . I want to nurture protest and lend fire to dissent. Without them a democracy perishes. Yet I want to avoid slipping into paranoia, destruction for its own sake, and the morbid malaise of hopelessness.

I want to build an intellectual spirit interlaced by commitment and capable of passion. Yet I do not want to succumb to the arrogance of mere fashion by denigrating authentic tradition and the goal of objectivity.

I want to respond to ideas instead of charismatic personalities whose programed chic (for whatever cause) is the product of exploitation.

I want to believe sincerely in the aspects of faith that undergird my life, yet also want to resist narrow chauvinism and self-righteous fanaticism that claims mine is the "only" faith or ideology, life style or system. I want to fight the conviction that "we" (people who share my views and I) are "good guys" versus "bad guys" (people who hold different views). . . .

. . . . I want to be a loyal and dependable (therefore always critical) member of movements and organizations to which I belong, yet do not want to forget that moral ambiguities mark all movements and institutions (including mine).

I want to participate in community with persons who share my views, yet do not want to lose the capacity for listening to totally different views and engaging in communication with people who hold them.

I want to be outspoken against the maladies and sins of my society, nation, and institutions, yet do not want to become merely a shrill crier of doom who offers no alternatives, decent hope for change, or positive approaches to hard and complex tasks.

So, I choose to live in creative tension. At the heart of creative tension, The Lover is present as Reconciler. . . .

. . . . Is The Lover inside or outside the church?

As a man who continues to stand within the framework of the institutional church, I have been one of its strong critics for a number of years. I shall continue to be outspoken in criticizing what I believe to be its failings. However, I also believe that we need the church—the emerging church, not an unchanged repository of old rituals and unquestioned creeds. These are my reasons.

First, the Judeo-Christian tradition is central to what is best in our experience. Too often it has been honored in name only while public as well as private morality has been tainted by blatant hypocrisy. Yet where social progress has been made or the authoritarian power of any abusive structure of the status quo seriously questioned, the Judeo-Christian tradition has provided a moral center from which action could emanate. A primary reservoir of this tradition is the church. If a breakdown in Christian corporate structure, with its historical and theological roots, should result in the isolation of privatized religious experience, individual consciences would be left to their own devices. . . .

. . . . "A man's home is his castle." This simplistic phrase has led many people into a fantasy world. It might be only a short jump from that to yet another simplistic phrase: "A man's home is his church." The danger of this lies in its threat of severely subjective moral judgments.

In worship restricted to one's home, sermons—if preached—would surely bestow blessings upon one's present path of life instead of questioning its integrity as weighed in the balance of the Word of God. Prayers would tend to lull a conscience instead of poking at, jabbing and needling it. . . .

. . . . Second, if privatized religious experience of churchless Christians should grow, there is the threat of a biblically and theologically illiterate new generation of people. Certain critics of organized religion might mockingly call this eventuality a boon instead of a threat. I disagree. Such illiteracy would only deepen the malaise of private and public alienation from society wherever it is found. It could also contribute to the possibility of a far more malignant development—a manufactured theology, unhinged from a moral center, and designed to serve as the harbinger of any racist demagogue, militaristic life style, or government-by-exploitation. . . .

. . . . I am astonished by the failure of the media to interpret the serious implications inherent in the phenomenon of churchless Christians. The absence of an institutional structure for ethics and moral behavior would produce an equivalent loss of guidelines for people trying to live meaningful lives in the midst of what often seems to be an urban-technological crossword puzzle. For example, a human person needs constant reminders that his "neighbor" is universal and legion, as well as inside the next apartment or house. The absence of guidelines and reminders could perpetuate a definition of "neighbor" as only someone living next door—and possibly having just the same color of skin, income, and cultural background. This would wipe out the profoundly Christian sense of "neighbor" as someone also living across town or halfway around the world, with perhaps a different color and culture, in need of nourishment or protection from persecution for a belief. Christian action—such as we have seen evidenced in civil rights, the peace movement, and acts of humanitarianism that have connected people across oceans and vast continents—calls for Christians to respond to the needs of a "neighbor" in the same sense as having a "brother." . . .

. . . . Presently many people are looking for pragmatic answers and depth of vision as they struggle seriously to make spiritual sense out of their lives. They are worried about drugs and crime, war atrocities and racial separatism, high taxes and overcrowded school classes for their children, ecological crises and politics, machines that break down and prices that spiral, security in old age and personal anguish in the face of a collapse of old beliefs. Most people today are not interested in a nineteenth-century answer to questions about faith or one out of an ancient church council. They want an answer that holds identifiable meaning for their lives in sexuality and work, politics and leisure, anxieties and happiness. . . .

. . . . The institutional church must come to understand what is happening in people's lives. I wonder when it will quit talking to itself and recognize the validity of people's current questions, as well as the honesty of many men and women who have left it. Already it is hard even to reach these people. They are fragmented. They are nondenominational. They have repudiated old forms of authority that spoke to them from high places concerning such matters as their attitudes toward dogmas, what they should or should not do in bed while lovemaking, or even if they might take a social drink. . . .

. . . . Their sharp reaction against institutional religion holds both promise and danger. At its best, it could offer a strong corrective to deadened forms of religion and issue in new forms directly related to people's lives. At its worst, it could obliterate any shared center of religious and even moral experience.

In the future, the emerging church may take forms that we cannot presently dream of. However, the sign of the essential church is that it steadily draws us outside our various ghettos (including religious ones) toward God and therefore close to other people in the world, not in an attitude of exploitation but of responsibility.

Third, we need the vision of the church. Without vision, we perish. We need windows opening out of the otherwise flat surfaces of our lives, giving us dimension. Instead of looking at a wall, we can try to open a window in it and see sky, clouds, earth, trees, flowers, animals, structures, and *people*. The church, at its best, reminds us that God became a man who entered into the world of *people*. . . .

. . . . Joy and laughter are essential parts of the human vision that must also comprehend darkness and tragedy. Peter L. Berger has spoken of power as "the final illusion while laughter reveals the final truth." Faith, hope, and love are not at all outworn realities even if they often seem to be outworn words. They are realities which enable us to persevere against both cruel circumstances and harsh depression, holding onto joy and laughter in our lives. All is not prosaic, humorless, or regimented. Life is a drama with color, music, lows, and highs.

We need the church with its sacraments to remind us again and again of the haunting quality of mystery in life. This affords us punctuation marks for the rituals of our own lives—birth, love, marriage, work, study, leisure, crisis, tragedy, and death. . . .

. . . . We need the vision of the emerging church to teach us, in every new generation, that unless we are willing to die to our selfishness and pride in actions of sacrifice and loving, we cannot truly mature and fully live.

We need this vision to show us prophets, those men and women in every age whose love is fired by a passion for justice that goads them to risk martyrdom itself for the sake of truth.

The true church is not simply a building on the corner of Second and Elm, although that edifice may house a bit of it. The true church is a thunderous shout of joy, a lamentation so loud that it fills valleys, and The Lover roaming the earth. The true church is bigger than any of us or our attempts to make it conform to our own image. Yet it also takes the occasional form of an intimate community—where two or three are gathered together in a sense of belonging to the universal body. The true church, constantly engaged in the process of emerging into human life, links us to judgment, healing, and love.

IX

I TALK TO THE LOVER ABOUT MYSELF, OTHER PEOPLE, AND
LIFE IN THE WORLD.

I CAN'T UNDERSTAND PROGRESS IN TERMS OF TALL NEW BUILDINGS, FASTER PLANES, OR TRIPS TO OUTER SPACE, WHEN PEOPLE STILL SUFFER FROM LACK OF FOOD, ARE DENIED EQUALITY, AND TORTURE ONE ANOTHER IN BODY, MIND, AND SPIRIT.

I can't understand why people want to place others on any kind of rack and twist them into unrecognizable and dehumanized forms. I can't understand why people want to tie other people's hands and then methodically administer the lash to their bleeding, lacerated backs, once, twice—ten times—twenty times—thirty times.

I can't understand why anybody wants to damage anyone else's mind or mortally wound his soul. Or why anybody wants to diminish anyone else's dignity or hurt him by denying him nourishment, education, housing, justice, or love.

Isn't equal opportunity an expression of love, while its denial is a tangible form of hate? Please help us to understand how indifference can be the most cruel form of hate.

There are times, I must confess, when I want to find an idyllic refuge, indulgently go my selfish way, and deny kinship with life outside my immediate concern. But my conscience won't go away or be comfortingly silent. It appears to be a very part of myself, like my arms, mind, and heart. It goes on speaking to me over and over again. It makes me hear the cries of innocent victims whose lives were brutalized and ground into the dust and whose blood calls for redress from the earth that I stand upon. Is it you speaking to me over and over again in my conscience?

Thank you for the sensitive, vulnerable, and courageous men and women who have given of themselves despite discouragement and danger for the sake of others—your saints in each generation.

Please help the rest of us not to give up the enduring struggle for human progress. Please warm our spirits when they have grown cold. Please open us up to one another when we seek to lock ourselves away in a ghetto of loneliness or a private place of hurt and despair.

Thank you for making us brothers and sisters to one another. Thank you for letting us see your face in the faces of the people around us.

Teach all of us to be lovers.

ABOUT MALCOLM BOYD . . .

The *Los Angeles Times* wrote about Malcolm Boyd: "He draws flak like a lightning rod draws zaps." "A spectacular example of the church's new thrust into secular life—a latter-day Luther or a more worldly Wesley," commented the *New York Times*. And the *Christian Science Monitor* wrote about Malcolm Boyd: "He is the saint of action," while *McCall's* stated: "Malcolm Boyd nourishes the spirit."

He received international recognition after the publication in 1965 of *Are You Running with Me, Jesus?* which has been hailed as a modern religious classic. The author of a dozen other books, he is also a playwright and has written theater and film criticism. Malcolm Boyd has long been identified as a leader in civil rights and the peace movement. An associate fellow in residence at Yale University in 1971–72, he has lectured on university campuses throughout the United States and Canada. Boston University has established The Malcolm Boyd Collection, a permanent archive of the priest-author's letters and papers.

Prior to his ordination as an Episcopal priest in 1955, Malcolm Boyd was a pioneer in television production and served as first president of the Television Producers Association of Hollywood. Following graduate theological training at Oxford University and Union Theological Seminary, he became rector of an inner-city parish in Indianapolis. Later he was a chaplain at Colorado State University and Wayne State University and served as a white assistant in black churches in Detroit and Washington, D.C.